The Legal Kiss

The Rule of Law Meets the Kiss

Victoria Sutton, M.P.A., Ph.D., J.D.
The Paul Whitfield Horn Professor
Texas Tech University School of Law

sutton.vickie@yahoo.com

Illustration and photography credits appear in the Bibliography

ISBN: 978-0-9838024-2-6

Printed in the U.S.A.

Typeset in the U.S.A.

Designed by Summer S. Sutton
Cover Illustration by Summer S. Sutton

Distributed in North America by Vargas Publishing

vargaspublishing.com

To Allan

Acknowledgement

The warmest thank you to Dennis E. Hackin
for his encouragement and comments and for introducing
me to ***Casablanca****, in his own, special way.*

A kiss is still a kiss
Casablanca
Herman Hupfeld, As Time Goes By (1942)
You must remember this
A kiss is still a kiss, a sigh is just a sigh
The fundamental things apply
As time goes by.

Thanks and kisses to my children,
Summer S. Sutton and Remington J. Sutton

Table of Contents

Introduction to the Legal Aspects of the Kiss

All the legislation in the world will not abolish kissing
----- Elinor Glyn

The passion and emotion evidenced by the kiss has profound and important consequences and implications in law anywhere on the globe, and it is driven by an invisible but real economy of need and desire. Perhaps Judges Richard A. Posner and Guido Calabresi would agree that it fits the economics theory of law better than one might believe, at first impression.

We spend about fourteen days in our lifetime in the activity of kissing, and it is not surprising that there is a history of attempting to legislate and regulate this pleasurable activity, and even use it to further the operation of the law. The idea of a kiss has also been a part of the rich idiomatic English language, and also finds a firm place in the legal history of the "kiss."

The idioms involving a "kiss" are plenty and for the British and Australians, to "give someone the kiss of life" is to help someone who has stopped breathing by blowing air into their mouth and rhythmically pressing the air back out by pressing on the chest. Then there is "kiss and tell" which ultimately leads to a breach of privacy or a breach of a confidentiality agreement or contract, when one of the parties discloses something that was thought to have been mutually agreed to keep private. To "kiss and make up" has also found its way into the law and could be used to describe the arbitration and mediation process, where the parties settle their disagreements (but perhaps don't stop being angry). A "kissing cousin" does not fit into the consanguinity charts of California or other states where inheritance is determined by the family tree charts, but it suggests a kind of informal familial relationship that may not have a basis in fact. Then, the "kiss it goodbye" idiom comes in rather handily to describe, for example, what happens when your star witness is turned into the star witness for your opponent, and there is a rather large sum of money at stake.

The more unpleasant idiom, "Kiss my Ass" seems to arise frequently in the law, often directed toward a judge. Its meaning is roughly a message to the recipient that they do not intend to do what they want you to do or they do not care for the recipient's position on an issue and wish them to take another, almost always, figuratively, that is. A slightly more Puritanical version is the "Kiss my foot," intended to purvey the same concept. This is very similar to the "Kiss off" idiom which is intended to send someone on their way in a disagreeable manner, minus the interaction with other body parts.

But returning to the more pleasant activity of the kiss, its legal history is rich with the foiables and the joys that its distraction brings to the participants, when either one or both are willing participants. Kissing while driving, kissing while being driven, kissing while giving legal advice, kissing while playing with guns, kissing while committing involuntary homicide, kissing as assault and battery, and false imprisonment while kissing are all part of this rich history. The kiss as a symbol, indeed an indica, of sexual harassment is a straightforward way of expressing aggression and rejection. The activity of kissing is so well understood that it can also indicate a state of mind, contribute to negligence, or be the proximate cause of an accident! The rich tradition of using the kiss in religious affirmations has been brought along into our arguably secular society where swearing and affirming one's beliefs to the government, at least at one time, involved kissing a Bible or other book.

As our understanding of public health increased

through the centuries, the kiss became a potentially regulated activity where the public health was at stake --- that is, the spread of disease caused by kissing was a basis for state regulation and prohibition of the offending conduct. At least one state has proscribed legally required warnings about kissing reptiles.

An infamous and high profile case reported in the New York Times in 1880, involved a gentleman who sought to enforce his oral contract (no pun intended) to receive kisses in exchange for property in a sale. The anomalies of state law and the rich history of addressing the activity of kissing are abundant. Countries rich in the tradition of regulating the kiss are not in short supply, and the visitor would do well to know about them!

The kiss as portrayed in the arts, in particular on the big screen, has led to censorship for its morally repugnant proposition and its negative influence on youth. Equally evoking emotion, is the idea that privacy is at stake where a couple is caught on camera in a passionate act of kissing, which becomes iconic. Not one, but two cases in two different countries were initiated for exactly this offense --- both wanted a part of the proceeds from the sales of their images.

The vagaries of the kiss are many, but this book is limited to its legal role, implications, or applications. To illustrate the complexity of "kissology", it should be noted that the French have at least twenty different kinds and the Germans have at least thirty. Kisses can be categorized in one of several categories, including kisses of love, affection, peace, respect, friendship as a symbolic religious act or as a symbolic legal act. The act of a kiss or even the thought of a kiss evokes emotion, and it is in law that one may find the manifestations of humankind's strongest emotions, sometimes played out with negligence, intent, malice, involuntarily, voluntarily, and sometimes, perversely.

This book is meant to be enjoyed, and does not seek to be a scholarly treatise on everything about the "kiss", but to focus quite simply on the legal aspects of the kiss in current jurisprudence as well as some parts of the legal history of the kiss, using the KISS principle, if you will pardon a pun, once again. The market for art depicting a kiss is sparked when the passionate embrace hits the mark and never seems to go out of fashion, illustrated by these three famous artforms: *The Kiss*, by Gustav Klimt (1907-1908); *The Kiss*, by Francesco Hayez (1859); and, *The Kiss*, by Rodin (1889).

The Kiss **(1907-1908)**
By Gustav Klimt

Kiss **(1859)**
By Francesco Hayez

This 19th century painting was unusual in that the action of kissing was not typically the subject of Western painting.

***The Kiss* (1889)**
By Rodin

The sculpture by Rodin depicts the passionate love of Francesca da Ramini and Paolo Malatesta, which grew as they read Lancelot and Buinevere together. The statue also depicts what led to a double murder of the adulterous couple by Francesca's outraged husband. (amazon.com)

Some Important Scientific Facts about Kissing

The scientific name for kissing is osculation, but the description from evolutionary psychologist, Gordon G. Gallup, defined a kiss for BBC, saying that it "involves a very compli cated exchange of information ---olfactory information, tactile information and postural types of adjustments that may tap into underlying evolved and unconscious mechanisms that enable people to make determinations . . . about the degree to which they are genetically incompatible." Interestingly, research bears this out, where in a recent Gallup survey, it was found that 59 percent of 58 men and 66 percent of 122 women admitted there had been times when they were attracted to someone, but the first kiss changed their minds.

Evolutionary biology would suggest that humans may not be the only animals who kiss, and indeed this seems to be the case. Some research indicates that the primate, Bonobos, practice a rather passionate form of kissing.

Lips seems to be the sensory center for making these important life determinations and are physiologically designed to do a good job of collecting data. The lips have one of the thinnest layers of skin on our body, and sensations on our lips are linked by five out of the 13 cranial nerves that affect cerebral function!

This physiological function would suggest that humans would engage in kissing quite naturally, and in fact that is true. From studies of human ethnology, researchers have found that 90% of the human population engages in kissing; yet more remarkable may be why the other 10% have not?

The Kissing Disease, and more

They say there's microbes in a kiss,
This rumor is most rife,
Come, lady dear, and make of me –
An invalid for life

---unknown author

Around the turn of the Twentieth Century when the Germ Theory was firmly embraced, the kiss lost some of its innocence. Kissing is associated specifically with several diseases. Mononucleosis is often called "the kissing disease" because it is carried in saliva and transferred during kissing or any exchange of saliva. The cause of cold sores, the *herpes simplex* 1 virus, is transmitted facilly during kissing. Other diseases are not associated as directly with kissing, but kissing has been implicated as a ready method of communicability for meningitis among teenagers. Although human immunodeficiency virus (HIV) can be transmitted through kissing, only one case of HIV has been reported to the Centers for Disease Control and Prevention that has been contracted through kissing.

Long before the Germ Theory was understood, during the 15th Century, in the clutches of the "Black Death" or the bubonic plague pandemic, it was suspected that it could be spread by kissing; thus, Henry VI banned kissing in England on July 16, 1439.

Kisses blown are kisses wasted.
Kisses aren't kisses unless they are tasted.
Kisses spread germs and germs are hated.
So kiss me baby; I'm vaccinated.

----unknown author

The Kiss: the sacred and the secular

[I kiss the soil] as if I placed a kiss on the hands of a mother, for the homeland is our earthly mother.

-----Pope John Paul II quotes
(Polish Pope. 1920-2005)

The kiss was considered to have both a secular and sacred effect for the ancient Hebrews, Greeks, and medieval Germans. Then, the kiss was used to designate and distinguish kin and family members from the rest of society.

One of the world's most famous kisses is undoubtedly the kiss of Judas Iscariot, which served to identify Jesus to the Roman soldiers in the Garden of Gethsemane. Judas famously accepted pieces of silver in exchange for this betrayal of Jesus, to whom he had served as one of his twelve disciples. In recognition of the power of the kiss, and its deadly mission on that day in Gethsemane, the early Christians abstained from kissing on the day commemorated as the Day of the Last Supper, Maundy Thursday. The "kiss of Judas" has found a permanent place in the English language as an idiom used to describe an act by a person who is betraying another.

The tradition of linking the secular with the sacred through the gesture of the kiss persisted among early Christians, and the kiss gained increasing recognition as an act of legal significance. Building upon the gesture of affection with close family and kin, the early Christians made the kiss an essential part of the ceremony for peace and unity in Christ. Expanding its use, it also became a legal rite which was intended to regulate property between marriage partners.

In the Second Century, the kiss was linked to liturgical acts of communal prayer and initiation rites, and by the Fourth Century, Eastern communities of faith were using the kiss in liturgies. The late Fourth Century included the kiss in close association with the Lord's Prayer and communion.

The Fourth Century may be the first emergence of the kiss as a legal instrument, used in the Roman pre-marriage contract, in part because secular law was reinforced by the relationship of the kiss in the religious function of the kiss. There was a legal bond that continued to develop with the kiss over the subsequent centuries.

In the Fifth Century, the kiss became the "holy kiss" and was increasingly used ceremonially. In a letter from Pope Innocent I to the Bishop of Gubbio, the kiss was linked to the communion and served as the 'closing seal or the assent of the congregation to the act of consecrating the mysteries,' which indicated the sanctity of the kiss.

The earliest extant evidence of the kiss as a legal instrument of the peace, according to Dr. Petkov, is in the legislation of Emperor Henry II in 1019. Also in the Eleventh Century, in trade of property between equals in Normandy, a seller would kiss the buyer or recipient of land to denote the legal transfer of the property, sealing the transaction. A kiss was also a practiced rite in the transfer of land or fealty from Lord to vassal, involving a full, on the mouth kiss, to make the vassal a "man of mouth and hands".

In England, July 16, 1439, King Henry VI banned the practice of kissing to combat the bubonic plague, otherwise known as the "Black Death." Long before the cause of bubonic plague was discovered, the kiss was suspect as a link to transmission. Certainly when the plague turned pneumonic, the King was dead right.

In the 1500s, the legal contract for peace was sealed by a kiss of peace. This physical act of emotion was coupled with the legal agreement to set aside feelings of anger, and Gregorio Lopez published the Spanish Code which described two ways to make peace: one was with words and embrace, and the other was with words and a kiss. Several cities in Italy also codified the use of the kiss of peace, with detailed regulations of the implications of this now, very legal act.

The photograph of the kiss of the sailor returning from World War II on V-J Day was one of the most famous photographs ever published by *Life Magazine*.

It was taken in Times Square by Alfred Eisenstaedt.

A Kiss is just a Kiss, except when it is worth a lot of money.

A kiss can be a comma, a question mark or an exclamation point.
----Mistinguett, the risqué French dancer, singer and actress

These passionate embraces punctuated with kisses which in these cases, are exclamation points, have sparked the emotions of the viewers of the photographs, but also sparked the emotions of the subjects in a different way. Two famous photographs that gained world attention, at two different times, drew their subjects and others into a frenzy of litigation to recover what they felt was rightfully their share of the financial gains from of their high profile breach of privacy.

V-J Day in Times Square

This memorable and passionate image of the return of a sailor on V-J Day, at the end of World War II, captured more than the hearts of the American public. To one man, this "capture" represented a misappropriation of his image for a commercial purpose. In *Mendonsa v. Time Incorporated*, 678 F. Supp. 967 (D.R.I. 1988), the man claiming to be the one in the photograph was seeking not only financial compensation but also recognition that he was the actual person in the photo delivering the passionate kiss.

The photograph was taken by Alfred Eisenstaedt, in Times Square, upon notice that the Japanese had surrendered. Eisenstaedt, once identified as the photographer of the century and described in the New York Times in 1954 as "a master of the little detail, the homely trifle, that tells a big story," cap-

Robert Doisneau's 1950 photograph "Le Baiser de l'Hotel de Ville"

tured the image after running to Times Square to take photographs as the announcement that the Japanese had surrendered was being broadcast. The photograph was published in the August 27, 1945 issue of *Life Magazine.*

However, the image was subsequently reprinted in the magazine, and in August 1980, the editors of *Life Magazine* published a request for individuals who believed they were depicted in the photograph to contact *Life Magazine.* George Mendonsa responded to the solicitation saying that he was the "kissing sailor." Then, in April 1987, *Life Magazine* published an advertisement, offering to sell copies of the photograph for $1,600 each, which undoubtedly led to the filing of a law suit under Rhode Island law, R.I.Gen.Laws § 9-1-28.1(a)(2) (1985), seeking compensatory damages and injunctive relief for "misappropriation of likeness" for "purposes of trade".

While it was clear that the first photograph of the passionate kiss was clearly newsworthy because it captured the American reaction to the Japanese surrender and the end of World War II, the subsequent republishing and marketing of the photograph by *Life Magazine* became "trade" under the "misappropriation of likeness" statute. The court dismissed the defendant's motion for failure to state a claim, and the plaintiff's case was allowed to go forward. However, George Mendonsa dropped the suit, because of the expense of litigation, never to be certified as the real "kissing sailor."

There were other claimants as well. Edith Shain, a nurse who had gone to Times Square upon the announcement of the Japanese surrender, claimed to be the nurse being kissed. She told a reporter fifty years after the photograph was published that, "You can imagine how people felt. They were just elated," she said. "Someone grabbed me and kissed me, and I let him because he fought for his country. I closed my eyes when I kissed him. I never saw him." Edith also told the reporter that she saw the photograph and recognized herself, but was embarrassed.

But how did Edith prove she was the nurse in the photograph? Her legs, of course. Eisenstaedt flew to Los Angeles, where Edith lived, to see if she was the person he had photographed, and as Edith relates the story to the reporter, "He looked at my legs and said I was the one."'

[From: J. Michael Kennedy, "The Kiss Seen "Round the World," The Los Angeles Times, 8/22/05 L.A. Times (Bus. Sec.).]

Le Baiser de l'Hotel de Ville

The dramatic cover photograph of a passionate kiss, symbolic of passion is placed in the city of renowned passion --- Paris. This story, too, proves that passion can also beget passion for litigation. The photograph, taken on April Fool's Day in 1950, was printed as a poster in 1986, and 410,000 copies were sold from 1986-1993. The theory of recovery for these financial gains was almost certainly inspired by the 1985 French Privacy Law, passed just prior to the release of the poster for sale, which was the foundation of the law suit filed in 1993. The plaintiffs, Denise and Jean-Louis Lavergne, claimed that they recognized themselves in the photograph taken by *Life Magazine* photographer Robert Doisneau, in 1950, and that he had invaded their privacy through this act of photography and publication, and they demanded compensation of $18,000. Plaintiff, Jean-Louis, claimed that he recognized the blue scarf gifted to him by his sister, and Plaintiff, Denise, still had the dress she was wearing that day. In addition, they produced a diary which proved they were together on that street on that very day, April Fool's Day, 1950. As if this was not enough for the court to consider, another plaintiff appeared to sue the photographer. Francoise Bornet claimed that she was the model in the photograph, and although she had been paid, it was only a small sum, and she should now be paid more, as well as future royalties. Her boyfriend had been the other half of the couple in the photograph, Jacques Carteaud, but he did not join in the law suit.

The court dismissed the Lavergnes case, finding that they were not the couple in the photograph, opining that the Lavergens, "had provided no proof of the illicit reproduction of their features." The court also dismissed the Bornet case, the case of the model against the photographer, finding although her claim "is not contested," that it was impossible to identify her in the photograph, because of the angle of her face, despite the evidence of the contact sheets produced by the agency which had acquired the model for Mr. Doisneau, and perhaps the most salient point, she had waited forty-three years to file her claim, far beyond a reasonable time. But Ms. Bornet may be the only party to have received financial compensation from the entire controversy when she sold an original print of the photograph sent to her by Doisneau with his autograph, for €155,000 Euros on April 25, 2005.

Jacques Carteaud noted that he had been paid 500 francs at the time, and he felt that was adequate compensation.

In general, singling out individuals who are kissing for a photograph can very well be a misappropriation of a likeness unless it is reporting a newsworthy event; however, if you wish to turn it into a profitable item for commercial trade, that kiss will definitely cost you.

The Celebrated Contractual Kisses

There is the kiss of welcome and of parting, the long, lingering, loving, present one; the stolen, or the mutual one; the kiss of love, of joy, and of sorrow; the seal of promise and receipt of fulfillment.

----Thomas C. Haliburton,
Canadian writer (1796-1865)

The case of *Finch v. Waters*, tried in a North Carolina County Court of Law in 1880, became a most celebrated case. The *New York Times* published an article, May 12, 1880, with the nondescript title, "An Important Case." There was some lack of reporting fact-checking at the time among the papers who reprinted the article, and the *New York Times* wrote that the case was *Finch v. Waters*; the *Irish Law Times* did the same; while the *Central Law Journal* wrote that the case was *Finch v. Walters*. Nonetheless, it was described by all as deciding the important question of whether kisses could form sufficient consideration for a contract, and what exactly was a "legal kiss"? The article from the *New York Times*, May 12, 1880, is reprinted below:

An Important Case

Some time ago Mr. Finch, of Newbern, who is in the jewelry business, exhibited to Miss Waters, a young lady with whom he was on friendly terms, a beautiful set of real jet. The lady was very anxious to own the set, but was not able to buy it. In these circumstances Mr. Finch proposed a novel kind of bargain. He said that he would sell Miss Waters the set for one hundred kisses, to be paid at the rate of one kiss daily on each and every dy next ensuing from the day of the date of the agreement, excepting, nevertheless, each and every Sunday thereafter. It was further provided that Mr.

Finch was to call at the lady's house every morning, except Sunday morning, to receive his daily kiss, which Miss Waters undertook and promised to duly deliver to him. This contract was not reduced to writing, but it was fully understood and agreed to by both parties, and the set of jet was tendered to Miss Waters and accepted by her.

The next morning Mr. Finch called on Miss Waters for his first kiss, which, as the young lady now maintains, was fully paid. On each subsequent morning for thirty consecutive days --- Sundays excepted --- the same proceedings were had. On the thirty-first day, however, Mr. Finch made a formal complaint that Miss Waters was not fulfilling her contract, inasmuch as she insisted upon permitting him to kiss her cheek only. He maintained that this did not constitute a legal kiss, and he demanded that he should be allowed to put his left arm around Miss Waters's waist and kiss her in the highest style of the art. To this request a firm refusal was returned. The lady professed her willingness to carry out her agreement, so far as he cheek was concerned, and even offered to give Mr. Finch his choice of cheeks, but she insisted that the contract would not bear the construction put upon it by Mr. Finch, and that she would never submit to such a construction. Thereupon, Mr. Finch, in great indignation, left the house, and brought an action for breach of contract against the lady.

This action raises several new and important questions, among the most important of which is, what constitutes, in the eye of the law, a kiss? The testimony of several experts is to be introduced by the plaintiff; but although these experts will probably start out with the assertion that a kiss is that which is impressed by one pair of lips upon another pair, they will subsequently be compelled to admit, on cross-examination that one pair of lips alone may imprint a kiss upon any accessible object. This seems, at first sight, fatal to the plaintiff's claim that the defendant did not furnish him with lawful current kisses, but it must be noted that he sets up the further plea that there is a difference between active and passive kisses; that Miss Waters promised to give him a certain quantity of kisses --- not to permit him to take them --- and that giving kisses is an act which requires the use of the lips. This is certainly a strong point, and though the court may decide that there is no one variety of kiss which can be held to be the only kiss known to the common law it may give an authoritative definition of an active kiss which will be of immense service to mankind. It is maintained by counsel for the defendant that there was no contract between the parties, for the reason that kisses can not constitute a valid consideration. The decision on this point will be eagerly waited for. That a kiss is something which can be given willingly or taken by force, and that it is commonly reputed to possess more or less intrinsic value, are points which the plaintiff's counsel will eloquently maintain. Hence it seems that a kiss may be a valuable and sufficient consideration upon which to base a contract. On the other hand, it is asserted that courts have never recognized a kiss as property capable of being stolen, and that when a kiss has been seized by violence the only remedy of the injured person is an action for assault. It is evident that we have here a question which admits of a vast amount of argument, and that its judicial decision will mark an era in our common law jurisprudence.

There is still another defence upon which defendant's counsel is understood to place great reliance. It is claimed that even if there was a valid contract between the parties, and if the defendant did break it, the plaintiff's proper remedy is not an action for a breach of contract, but a bill in equity for specific performance. Probably the plaintiff would have been wise had he resorted to the latter course. In case of his success, he would then have received specified quantities of definite kisses of one kind or another, and would thus have gained a substantial victory. As it is, his triumph in his action for breach of contract would doubtless bring him only a nominal sum by way of damages, and would render it necessary for him to institute fresh proceedings in order to gain possession of the jewelry. Still, it by no means follows that because he may have a remedy in equity he has no remedy at law, and it is reasonably certain that if there was a contract between himself and the defendant an action for breach of it will lie.

There are man ignorant persons who fancy that the law is

a dry, prosaic business. This action, however, proves the contrary. The questions at issue in Finch v. Waters *come home to every mouth in the country. There is at present almost lamentable vagueness of belief as to what constitutes a kiss, and as to its precise legal status. We shall now have these questions decided, and the social interests of the community cannot fail to be vastly benefited thereby.*

The *Central Law Journal* and the *Irish Law Times*, included the story in its entirety, in their editions in 1880. The case was not reported through the state reporter, and the archives of Craven County, where New Bern is located, has lost track of this "most important case" archive.

The legal question raised by this case is whether a kiss can be sufficient consideration in a contract, and what we wish to know, is what exactly constitutes a "legal kiss"? Perhaps more important to Mr. Finch, we do not know if he was able to secure specific performance on his contract. The courts have held that the 13th Amendment, U.S. Constitution, prohibits the specific performance of personal services such as an employment agreement, being a condemnation to servitude, i.e., slavery. Perhaps this would lead us to conclude that such a contract as this one is unenforceable because kisses are not valuable consideration, after all. Perhaps the court *sua sponte* may have decided that the proper remedy was simply to put the parties back into the same position in which they find themselves, before the fateful transaction?

Today, if we checked the Restatement (Second) of Contracts (2008), Chapter 4. Formation Of Contracts—Consideration; Topic 1. The Requirement Of Consideration; § 71. Requirement Of Exchange; Types Of Exchange, we might agree that a kiss is "an act other than a promise" as outlined on the following page:

(1) To constitute consideration, a performance or a return promise must be bargained for.
(2) A performance or return promise is bargained for if it is sought by the promisor in exchange for his promise and is given by the promisee in exchange for that promise.
(3) The performance may consist of
(a) an act other than a promise, or
(b) a forbearance, or
(c) the creation, modification, or destruction of a legal relation.
(4) The performance or return promise may be given to the promisor or to some other person. It may be given by the promisee or by some other person.

The Restatement (Second) of Contracts; § 79. Adequacy Of Consideration; Mutuality Of Obligation; concludes that *if the requirement of consideration is met, there is no additional requirement of*

(a) a gain, advantage, or benefit to the promisor or a loss, disadvantage, or detriment to the promisee; or
(b) equivalence in the values exchanged; or
(c) "mutuality of obligation."

From these references, coming in the century-plus which followed this case, our legal scholars of the American Law Institute have resolved the issue of consideration, but Constitutional jurisprudence of the 13th Amendment teaches us that it is unenforceable as specific performance. Perhaps the most burning question which has gone unanswered, still, is what is a "legal kiss"?

Kisses and the Konstitution [sic]

Kiss me. Kiss me as if it were the last time.
---*Casablanca* (1942), Ilsa to Rick

Movies as free expression are protected by the First Amendment, U.S. Constitution, and the use of any prior restraint in this expression of free speech, must be carefully considered in terms of what is the compelling government interest weighed against the fundamental right of free speech, in freely showing the film. The value of the free speech is also part of the equation, and depicted behaviors which do not have high value, do not receive the highest protection of their expression. So the depiction of a kiss could fall into a category of low value where some restrictions of its expression may be constitutionally permissible.

The United States Supreme Court has spoken on this issue of whether movies can be subject to prior restraint. In a landmark case, the U.S. Supreme Court reviewed a challenge to the City of Chicago's prior restraint law, that all films had to be submitted to the censor before they could be shown in the city. In this case, the Petitioner, New York Corporation, owned the rights to the movie, *Don Juan*, and applied for a permit to the City of Chicago Police Commissioner in accordance with the ordinance which read: . . .*permit shall be granted only after the motion picture film for which said permit is requested has been produced at the office of the commissioner of police for examination. . .* The permit was not granted, but it was because the Petitioner refused to submit the film for review. In *Times Film Corp. v. City of Chicago*, 365 U.S. 43 (1961), the court wrote that *motion pictures are included within the free speech and free press guaranties of the First and Fourteenth Amendments, [and] there is no absolute freedom to exhibit publicly, at least once, every kind of motion picture*, 365 U. S. at 46, 49-50. However, the court held that an ordinance requiring submission of films prior to showing in the city does not constitute, on its face, a prior restraint within the prohibition of the First and Fourteenth Amendments. That is, ordinances like the City of Chicago's prior restraint ordinance was not unconstitutional merely because it was a prior restraint.

In the U.S. Supreme Court opinion, reference is made to a Pennsylvania censor who upon reviewing the movie, *Carmen*, found it to be objectionable because of the "duration of a kiss." 365 U.S. at 72. Cecil B. DeMille noted in 1921 that all thirty-five state and municipal censoring bureaus demanded alterations to *Carmen*, and unfortunately, no two demanded the same change. In the case of Pennsylvania, they demanded that the duration of the kiss be reduced to "a mere snippet of five feet of film", which forced the viewers in southern New Jersey, although not censored themselves, to watch the Pennsylvania-approved, five-foot version of the kiss. [William Bruce Johnson, *Miracles and Sacrilege: Roberto Rossellini, the Church, and Film Censorship in Hollywood* (Univ of Toronto Press, 2008) at p. 93.]

Fortunately, by 1942, Rick was allowed to kiss Ilsa "as if it were the last time," in *Casablanca* which has been voted the number one, most romantic movie of all time, by the American Film Institute.

Is a Kiss "any other valuable inducement" in elections?

What does it avail now of promising votes,
For a Devonshire kiss in an instant turns coats,
Besides lay a wager of five guineas to boot,
You surely win, kiss again, bring him in .

----*The Countryman's Frolick; or Humours of an Election* (May 14 1784)

It cannot be disputed that baby-kissing is a practice of the ardent politician, at least in the West, and photographs of these kisses are often portraying the politician as caring, sensitive, and adoring. This practice may have been officially born in Charles Dickens, *The Pickwick Papers* (1836), depicting the Eatanswill election, when the candidate, Samuel Slumkey, is told by his agent that he should kiss the babies after he has patted them on the head. To this he replies, "*'Very well,' said the honoroùable Samuel Slumkey, with a resigned air, 'then it must be done. That's all.'*"

In 1977, following the new campaign contribution limitation of $1,000, satirist Tom Wolfe quipped that "more than ever, people in show business have a tremendous role in campaigns. Through concerts and other entertainments they can deliver a million dollars in a single evening, and in show business, this kissing has become even more rampant than it ever was. Jimmy Carter has to kiss at least 3,000 rock stars—male and female—in the next four years to pay up his debt."

The elections of the 18th Century were much less discrete with their show of affections, and bely the Victoria myth of sensibilities to overt shows of emotion. Through the 1700s, the activity of electioneering kissing was practiced where the women as well as the men utilized the activity for procuring commitments to vote for their candidate. It was even a social status symbol, because poorer women could be bought with small payments, whereas the more elite class of women could not be persuaded to shape their husband's and brothers' votes with trivial, small payments, and the kiss served the purpose of lacking this crass, cash value, yet it had value. The use of the kiss in electioneering was never seen as corrupting in these circumstances. This rampant behavior was depicted in the Trusler farce of a county election, where the candidate, during his kiss, transfers a guinea from his mouth to the mouth of the wife of a land freeholder, in order to procure his vote.

This balance of female influence over the males during an election, who otherwise were deprived of the right to vote, was satisfactory to Victoria society, until women became more involved. In 1784, the Duchess of Devonshire became involved in the Westminister election and was credited with procuring the victory for Charles James Fox through her electioneering kisses. This made the press and public more apprehensive about the corruptible possibilities from the electioneering kiss. Kissing itself was not considered corruption, but it did factor into the depositions held by the Members of Parliament who heard disputed election cases in the English courts of the 1700s.

Avoiding bribery in elections, however, remains a threat to democracy, and there is a delicate balance in encouraging people to vote and coercively or wrongly influencing their vote. As a practice, campaigns have typically provided punch and cookies and various trinkets for promoting their candidates, and this has been an acceptable kind of promotion that does not rise to the level of bribery.

In general, U.S. election law on these token gifts and treats is stated this way:

> *It is generally held that treating by a candidate, as is customarily done in the daily intercourse of men, is not a violation of a corrupt-practices act, or a similar act, prohibiting the influencing of voters by the gift of refreshments.* 26 Am Jur 2d Elections § 380 (1996).

Another important factor in bribery in elections is that most of the regulation is at the state and local level, not the federal level. At the federal level, the applicable law prohibiting *illegal inducement* and punishment by the Federal Election Commission at 42 U.S.C. § 1973(i)(c) applies only to elections involving federal candidates.

At the state level, each state is free to develop their own statutes to address illegal inducement. The Alaska illegal inducement statute, AS § 15.56.030(a)(2), goes so far as to allow payments for inducement to vote, which would not rise to the level of illegal inducement. The Alaska statute does not *prohibit payment to induce persons to vote who would not otherwise do so, so long as they are not induced to vote in a particular manner.*

The Ohio illegal inducement statute, Ohio Revised Code § 3599.01, prohibits any person to *give, lend, offer, procure or promise to give, lend offer, or procure any money, office, position, place or employment, influence or any other valuable consideration to or for a delegate, elector, or other person.* [emphasis added]. This statute is read to be much broader and would almost certainly sweep in the possibility of using kisses as an inducement to the extent kisses may be determined to be "valuable consideration".

California, in a clear policy statement to encourage voters to vote, permits voters to receive incentives for voting at Cal. Elec. Code. § 18522(a)(1996)).

Oregon's illegal inducement statute has been interpreted by their court which provided this guidance for determining whether the inducement rises to the level of being illegal: *In order to induce a person to vote, one must promise or provide something beyond which is involved in the act of voting; there must be an advantage which has independent value to the voter. Otherwise it could not induce the decision to vote.* Oregon Rep. Party v. State, 78 Or. App. 601, 604-05 (Or. App. 1986).

Then, would kisses be an acceptable inducement to vote, and not an illegal inducement? At least in Alaska, a payment to induce someone to vote is acceptable --- which might open the door to kisses --- as long as the kisses do not cause the voters *to be induced to vote in a particular manner*; whereas, caution may be advised in Ohio, where *any other valuable consideration* from a person may be illegal inducement, as well as in Oregon. California may consider kisses to be acceptable incentives.

Perhaps the U.S. Supreme Court might wish to sort out this conflicting and unclear collection of state voting law [For cases where the U.S. Supreme Court will opine on state voting law questions, see Bush v. Gore, 531 U.S.98 (2000).] if a "Kissing Gate" arises. "Hanging Chads" can't be more interesting than kisses for votes!

THE DEVONSHIRE, or Most Approved Method of Securing Votes

Kiss and Tell

O fie, miss, you must not kiss and tell.
--- William Congreve, *Love for Love* (1695)

The problem of "kiss and tell" should be carefully considered well in advance of assuming the risk of private disclosures that may cause emotional distress. Indeed, disclosures of private information in a tort claim would make a claim for emotional distress damages; yet, it is possible to develop a contractual agreement intended to ensure the confidentiality between two partners.

A sample confidentiality agreement suggests that the parties agree that they will not disclose private information because to do so, will likely result in damages from emotional distress. Here is the sample agreement:

Sample Confidentiality Agreement for Intimate Partners

The undersigned parties, for the valuable consideration of society, companionship, and all of the other many services and benefits mutually conferred by intimate partners, enter into this agreement of confidentiality as part of an intimate relationship that they have established. The parties agree it is essential to their quest for emotional, spiritual, and physical intimacy that private information and acts that communicate private information be shared and take place in an atmosphere of mutual trust in which each party can rely on the other not to disclose to third parties private, embarrassing information about the other acquired in the course of the relationship. "Private, embarrassing information" is to be given a common sense construction in accordance with ordinary standards of decency and general understanding. The term includes information relating to mental and physical health, sexual activities, personal finances, quirks and eccentricities, indiscretions, and immodest or sexually oriented photographs or video in any format. It is expressly understood that the object of this agreement is to protect emotional security and reputation. The parties agree that the most likely damages to result from a breach of the agreement will be in the nature of emotional distress.

Kiss and Tell: Protecting Intimate Relationship Privacy Through Implied Contracts of Confidentiality, 74 UCINLR 887 (Spring 2006).

Tell, before you kiss, may be the best advice if the party has *herpes simplex* I or human *papillomavirus* (HPV). Not all courts recognize a tort claim for the transmission of herpes and human *papillomavirus*, but Missouri and California courts have recognized one. So in privacy matters, the court has found that the interest in disclosure of the risk of contracting a disease had by a partner outweighs the individual privacy interest. Even in tort law, the objective is to discourage unsafe behavior, undercutting an argument for a higher right in protecting one's privacy and the incidental burden in disclosure.

In *Deuschle v. Jobe*, 428 N.W.2d 103 (Minn. Ct. App.

1988), the Missouri Court of Appeals for the Western District of Missouri took a significant step by acknowledging an unmarried sexual partner's right to bring negligence and intentional tort claims for the transmission of these sexually transmitted diseases (STDs). The California court in *Doe v. Roe*, 267 Cal. Rptr. 564, 567 (Cal. App. 1990), held that where a sex partner was negligent in the transmission of *herpes* to a former partner, "it is beyond question that our state's policy of preventing the spread of venereal disease is great and that the burden of warning a prospective sex partner is small," holding that "(t)he incidental burden on (the) defendant in forcing him to disclose details of his sex life is not sufficient to outweigh the strong interest of the state in preventing the spread of communicable sexual diseases. Consequently[,] we find no constitutional infirmity in the judgment." Both courts found negligence in failure to disclose the defendant's disease.

In the case of herpes and HPV, the rule must then be, tell and then kiss (maybe).

The Forbidden Kiss: Indiscriminate Gender Kissing

Let him kiss me with the kisses of his mouth:
for thy love is better than wine.

---Song of Solomon 1: 1,
The Bible

The condemnation of homosexual conduct in public and sodomy in private by both homosexuals and heterosexuals has been enforced by laws for centuries. The earliest English law against sodomy was the Fleta of 1300, which reads that those who "are guilty of bestiality or sodomy shall be buried alive in the ground." The great legal commentator, Sir William Blackstone, references the importance of sodomy laws because of the unique destruction of Sodom and Gomorrah. In 1769, in the Commentaries, he wrote, "the express law of God, determine[s] [the crime of sodomy] to be capital. Of which we have a single instance ... by the destruction of two cities by fire from heaven." In the United States, by 1787 when the Constitution was ratified, all states had sodomy laws, and all but one had the death penalty for the crime, taking the import of the crime from Sir Blackstone.

The two landmark cases, cited in reference to same-sex regulation begin with *Bowers v. Hardwick*, 478 U.S. 186 (1986) when the U.S. Supreme Court ruled that sodomy can be prohibited because it is not a fundamental right. Seventeen years later, the U.S. Supreme Court expressly overrated *Bowers* whereas in *Lawrence v. Texas*, 539 U.S. 558 (2003), that a Texas law was violative of constitutional due process, infringing on a liberty interest of conduct in the home, of the most intimate kind. The sodomy law in Texas was specifically prohibited for homosexuals, but not for heterosexuals, and the parties were homosexuals, but not for heterosexuals, and the parties were engaged in the conduct in the privacy of a home, all in violation of 14th Amendment, substantive due process. As a result, this opinion invalidated the remaining 15 states' sodomy laws.

Visitors to inmates who were homosexual demanded that the prison in Arizona change their policy to allow homosexual partners to kiss, the same as the policy allows heterosexuals to kiss. In *Whitmire v. State of Arizona*, No. CV 98-0641, the Arizona policy was challenged, and they argued that it was a matter of safety. That is, if other prisoners observe that another prisoner is homosexual, that will potentially threaten the safety of that prisoner. Upon review, the Ninth Circuit, U.S. Court of Appeals did not find that logic compelling, reasoning that if they did not want to reveal their sexual preference then they did not have to engage in kissing during a visit.

Kissing has also been a factor in determining visitation rights of homosexual and lesbian partners and parents. In general, the law of *Custody and Visitation of Children By Gay and Lesbian Parents*, 64 AMJUR POF 3d 403, finds that the law has been unfavorable for partners who kiss in front of the children during visitations or custody. In *Pulliam v. Smith*, 348 N.C. 616, 501 S.E.2d 898 (1998), the court found that male homosexuals who kissed in view of the children caused psychological harm to the children, and in *Dailey v. Dailey*, 635 S.W.2d 391 (Tenn. Ct. App. 1981), the court found that lesbians who "kissed passionately" in front of the child had an adverse effect on the children.

State laws applying to kissing in public, for example, would have to apply equally to homosexuals and heterosexuals, following *Lawrence v. Texas*, and the parties were engaged in conduct in the privacy of a home, all in violation of 14th Amendment, substantive due process. As a result this opinion invalidated the remaining 15 states' sodomy laws.

So what does this mean for homosexuals kissing in public? State and local laws applying to kissing in public, for example, would have to apply equally to homosexuals and heterosexuals, probably before, but certainly after *Lawrence v. Texas*.

Newly appointed Secretary of State James F. Byrnes kissing the Bible at the swearing in ceremony as President Harry S. Truman watches.

Location: Washington, DC, US
Date taken: July 1945
Photographer: George Skadding
Life Magazine

Kiss the Bible, or not

An honest answer is like a kiss on the lips.
---Proverb 24:26

The Rule of Law is served by a procedural system which provides predictability and certainty of fair and equitable treatment to all citizens, and it follows that courts which are the guardians of the Rule of Law, would require order. That order, has always had a certain amount of ceremony, and one of those important features is the act of swearing to tell the truth in a court of law. Swearing ceremonies similarly conducted under the Rule of Law are those which require an oath of loyalty to serve as an employee, elected, or appointed official of the federal or states' governments, or to be admitted to citizenship into a country. The kiss has been a part of this rich and vibrate history of ceremony that continues to this day, at least in its recognition as a former part of the legal rite of the oath.

The symbolism of the kiss had been combined with many other legal instruments as part of the rule of law by the 13th and 14th centuries. The kiss was combined with seals, written records, as well as oaths and affirmations.

In the 1800s, the act of kissing the Bible when being sworn had become a rule riddled with exceptions. The act of being sworn often included not only a hand on the Bible while taking an oath but also a kiss to the Bible as a legal requirement.

In E. Cobham Brewer's *Dictionary of Phrase and Fable*, published in 1898, he includes this entry, "Kiss the Book":

Kiss the Book.

After taking a legal oath, we are commanded to kiss the book, which in our English courts is the New Testament, except when Jews "are sworn in." This is the kiss of confirmation or promise to act in accordance with the words of the oath (Moravians and Quakers are not required to take legal oaths). The kiss, in this case, is a public acknowledgment that you adore the deity whose book you kiss, as a worshipper.

It is now permitted to affirm, if persons like to do so. Mr. Bradlaugh refused to take an oath, and after some years of contention the law was altered.

Several states have notable statutes which specifically address the custom of kissing the Bible and affirmatively assure that the inductee is not required, or asked, to kiss the Bible or "Gospels", nor are they required to place their hand on the Bible. Illinois, 5 ILCS 255/3, specifically states that inductees shall not be compelled to *kiss the gospels*, and Massachusetts, Mass. Gen. Laws Ann. ch.233, § 15, similarly prohibits a requirement of kissing the gospels.

New Jersey and Virginia, somewhat less interested in moving away from the tradition of placing a hand on the Bible, still require that this be done; however, neither require that the inductee kiss the Bible. Virginia, at Va. Code Ann. § 49-10, stipulates that a person being sworn may be required to place their hand on the Holy Bible, but no one shall *require or request* any person *to kiss the Holy Bible or any book or books thereof.* The entire text reads as follows:

Title 49. Oaths, Affirmations and Bonds
Chapter 1. Oaths and Affirmations (Refs & Annos)
§ 49-10. Use of Bible in administration of oaths.
No officer of this Commonwealth, or any political subdivision thereof, shall, in administering an oath in pursuance of law, require or request any person taking the oath to kiss the Holy Bible, or any book or books thereof, but persons being sworn for any purpose may be required to place their hand on the Holy Bible.

Any officer in Virginia who violates the strict limitations of the oath giving process will be fined $100.

New Jersey, at N.J.S.A. 41:1-4, probably has the most interesting of all the selected statutes because although it does not require "the person taking the oath to kiss the holy scriptures, it is very specific in that putting a hand on the book would be sufficient, and the final sentence which includes the penalty maintains all of the significance of the kiss, which seemed to be ejected by all of the previous language of the statute. The final sentence makes clear the significance of the kiss and substitutes the hand on the Bible as a proxy for the kiss: *If any persons so sworn shall swear falsely they shall be guilty of perjury as though the book had been kissed. Here is the section in full:*

New Jersey, at N.J.S.A. 41:1-4
Title 41. Oaths and Affidavits
Chapter 1. Forms, Solemnities and Requisites of Oaths and Affidavits
41:1-4. Oath taken with hand on instead of kissing scriptures

It shall not be necessary to the solemnity or obligation of an oath administered in any court of justice or any legal proceeding, civil or criminal, in this state, for the person taking the oath to kiss the holy scriptures, but the taking of such oath, while the hand shall be held upon the book, shall answer all the purposes and requirements of the law, any usage or custom to the contrary heretofore notwithstanding. If any persons so sworn shall swear falsely they shall be guilty of perjury as though the book had been kissed.

The hand on the Bible has now become the final remnant of the ceremony of swearing an oath, and during the second swearing-in ceremony during the inauguration of President Obama, there was wide criticism that on the second ceremony, to correct the constitutional textual mix-up, that he had not taken the oath the second time, with his hand on the Bible. Even during his campaign, the rapidly circulating rumor that he would place his hand on the Koran became a minor campaign issue for a time, until after a great deal of explanation, the misconception that Barack Obama was a Muslim, was addressed.

It is clear that placing a hand on the Bible, which may be considered a modern day proxy for the kiss, is still a very important process for the American public.

Ukrainian President Viktor Yushchenko kisses the Bible after taking the oath of office during his inauguration ceremony at the parliament hall in Kiev, Jan. 23, 2005.

Order in the Court

Teach not thy lip such scorn, for it was made
For kissing, lady, not for such contempt.
---William Shakespeare

Many references and idioms involving kisses have been used in court, but sometimes, a genuine kiss can cause a disruption in court decorum, distracting from the court's role as guardian of the Rule of Law.

For example, in California, the California appeals court held that the trial court had acted properly by denying a motion for a mistrial where one male juror was "blowing kisses, winking [and] waving" to an Assistant U.S. Attorney. *United States v. Widgery*, 636 F.2d 200 (8th CIR.1980).

In a case in Missouri, a criminal defendant requested a rehearing because of the language used by the Prosecutor in characterizing the alleged criminal conduct of the defendant, and using frequent references to the Bible. In particular, the Defendant took offense that the Prosecutor argued that the defendant had placed her own kiss of Judas on her son. The court denied the rehearing, but cautioned that excessive Biblical references should not be made. *State v. Phillips,* 940 S.W.2d 512 (Mo. 1997).

The group of cases which follow describe another disruption of court decorum, with the use of the idiom, "Kiss my Ass," which is generally deemed inappropriate for the courtroom, unless it is presented as evidence. In Ohio, a defendant asked for a new trial, saying that when the Prosecutor told his defense counsel to "kiss [his] ass", he was denied a fair trial. The court denied his motion for a new trial, finding the Defendant was not denied a fair trial, but the court did write in dicta that the use of this language by the Prosecutor was "unprofessional." *State/City of Mason v. Stafford*, No. CA2001-08-079, 2002-Ohio-4710, 2002 WL 31008830 (12th Dist. Ct. App., 9-09-02).

In a South Carolina case, the Defendant had violated the terms of probation, and the court revoked her probation and re-instated her suspended, five-year sentence. The probation officer was tasked with having the Defendant sign the probation order, to which she signed it, "Kiss My Ass" and asked the probation officer to return it to the judge. Not surprisingly, the judge scheduled a contempt hearing within hours and found her in contempt of court, adding another 90-days to her sentence. *State v. Law*, Unpublished Opin. No. 2007-UP-557 (S.C. 2007).

But the most infamous motion was one filed in the Federal District court, Southern District of Georgia, entitled, "Motion to Kiss My Ass" by the Plaintiff, Matthew Washington, who was representing himself. The motion filed by Mr. Washington was one in which he moved "all Americans at large and one corrupt Judge Smith [to] kiss my got [sic] damn ass sorry mother fucker you." *Washington v. Judge Alaimo*, 934 F. Supp. 1395 (S.D. Ga. 1996). The court entered an order in response to this motion, citing Federal Rule of Civil Procedure 11, which addresses misconduct, that the Defendant would be required to file a contempt bond with the court and pay the filing fee before filing any further motions.

The Unwanted Kiss

A legal kiss is never as good as a stolen one.
-------Guy de Maupassant

The unwanted kiss can often be found in the company of the vilest of murders, sexual crimes, sexual harassment, pediphilia, and child molestation to list a few (and please note that necrophilia is not part of this list). However, the unwanted kiss in this section is defined as between two children or two adults, one of which has unfortunately misunderstood, miscommunicated, or anti-socially ignored all respectable social signals, and forged ahead with intentions to execute a kiss, and accomplished the mission.

The legal roots for the unwanted kiss come from the right of privacy, and the right of privacy is arguably found in natural law, as a basic human need, which should be protected by law in a civil society.

In tort law, it is clear that an unwanted kiss is a battery. The Restatement of Torts (First) uses the illustration of a kiss as follows: "1. A proposes to kiss B. B neither resists nor protests by word or gesture. A kisses B. A is not liable to B." The section from Division 1. Intentional Harms To Persons, Land And Chattels; Chapter 3. Privilege Arising From Consent To Intended Invasions Of Interests Of Personality; § 50. Actual and Apparent Assent describes the kind of assent (and the comment describes both action and inaction of concern) required to avoid tortuous battery:

(1) An actual assent is given by words or

conduct which are intended to express a willingness to submit to the invasion and are so understood by the person invading the interest.

2) An apparent assent is given by words or conduct which, while not intended to express a willingness to submit to the invasion, would be understood by a reasonable man to be so intended and are so understood by the person invading the interest.

Comment:
a. Action and inaction. Either an actual or apparent assent may be given by words or acts or by words and acts. Actions often speak louder than words. If a dentist tells a patient that a particular tooth needs filling and asks him to sit in the chair so that this may be done, the other's so doing is as complete an assent to the filling of the tooth as though he had expressed his willingness in words. Inaction may amount to an expression of willingness. The failure to resist or protest against an act apparently intended to invade one's interest of personality, or necessarily involving such an invasion, is conduct expressing apparent assent if one is aware of the threatened invasion and is capable of resistance or protest and the circumstances are such that a reasonable man would, and the person invading the interest does, understand the failure to resist or protest as expressing assent.

As we see from this description, and the example, inaction ---"failure to resist or protest" --- is just as functional as action, in signifying assent.

In *Craig v. M & O Agencies, Inc.*, 496 F.3d 1047 (9th Cir. 2007), an employee was followed into the ladies' restroom by her supervisor who gave her a kiss. The court held that this was an "unwelcome offensive touching" and thus constituted assault and battery, consistent with 6 Am. Jur. 2d Assault and Battery § 8. This, then, describes the legal definition of an unwanted kiss, when it is assault and battery in tort.

Sovereign immunity is quite a different matter when it involves the government as a party-defendant. In sovereign immunity cases, a typical statute, like M.S.A. § 176.031 *Employer's liability exclusive*, will govern which acts of employees are covered by the tort claims act against the government. In this case in Minnesota, in *Johnson v. Ramsey County*, 424 N.W.2d 800 (Minn. Ct. App. 1988), an employee received an unwanted kiss from the judge for whom she worked, but the court found no battery because although it happened at work, they opined, "that kiss had no association with the job and thus did not arise out of and in the course of employment."

Assault and battery from unwanted kisses --- that unwelcome offensive touching—can also appear with another tort claim, unlawful restraint, or false imprisonment. This can be a tort claim or a criminal charge, just as assault and battery.

In Ohio, the unlawful restraint criminal statute, R.C. § 2905.03 Unlawful restraint, requires, to be convicted under this statute:

> *(A) No person, without privilege to do so, shall knowingly restrain another of the other person's liberty.*

(B) No person, without privilege to do so and with a sexual motivation, shall knowingly restrain another of the other person's liberty.
(C) Whoever violates this section is guilty of unlawful restraint, a misdemeanor of the third degree.

In Ohio, in *State v. Beachy* (Ohio App. 5 Dist., Stark, 09-03-2002) No. 2001CA00339, 2002-Ohio-4714), a victim testified that the defendant had "held her shoulders and asked for a kiss" causing for that moment, unlawful restraint. When the defendant sought to appeal the conviction from the Municipal Court, which was a third degree misdeameanor, the appeals court found that he was not entitled to an acquittal.

Where the common law tort system has failed to redress unwanted kisses from an employer, some states have developed human rights statutes, such as the state of Washington. The statute, RCWA 49.60.180. Unfair practices of employers; 90. Casual, isolated, or trivial incidents, sexual harassment, when put to the test, did not redress the problem of an unwanted kiss, when that kiss was an isolated, one time occurrence. In *MacDonald v. Korum Ford*, 80 Wash.App. 877, 912 P.2d 1052 (1996), a manager kissed an employee at a party. Though admittedly offensive and inappropriate, it failed to rise to the level of an unfair practice of an employer under the human rights commission statute because it was an isolated event, with no other instances of inappropriate treatment of the employee.

Finally, where professionals abuse their position of trust with their patients and clients – in this case demanding kisses from them --- the protection of society will outweigh their privileges to practice their profession.

A physician, who made it a practice to exact kisses from

his female patients in exchange for prescriptions, found himself on trial for involuntary manslaughter for his grossly negligent manner of prescribing drugs to the victim. The physician sought to appeal his conviction for involuntary manslaughter, because his practice of exacting kisses was not relevant to the case at bar, and he argued that he could not have received an unbiased decision from the jury. However, on appeal the court noted that the trial judge "specifically advised jury that defendant was not on trial for "moral purposes" and that they should not allow their moral assessment of defendant to prejudice their determination of culpability," and this was sufficient. Further, the evidence was admission to establish a "course of conduct" in the manner in which the physician wrote prescriptions. His conviction of involuntary manslaughter, 18 Pa.C.S.A. § 2504 involuntary manslaughter, was affirmed. *Com. v. Youngkin*, 427 A.2d 285 (1981), 1356 Pa.Super. 417.

In the case of a military attorney, *Re Bellino* (1992, SC) 417 SE2n 535, who used force to take liberties with two female clients who he outranked in the military, his punishment was a suspension from the practice of law for six months and an additional 31 months of temporary suspension with the added requirement of taking the Professional Responsibility Examination. The military attorney had pulled the women toward him in attempts to kiss them in his law office, where they had come seeking his legal advice.

These cases involving unwanted kisses from employers and supervisors directed toward subordinates, using a tort theory of assault and battery, false imprisonment, or unlawful restraint, as we see, have failed where the employee is not acting in the scope of his or her duties, when they deviate for personal purposes to plant a kiss. Recognizing this flaw in the common law tort framework, a federal law was required to redress injuries from employers who are involved with sexual harassment of subordinates, or others under their control.

Title IX, 20 U.S.C. § 1681(a), provides for the protection of people in the United States in education programs or activities which receive federal funds. *Davis Next Friend LaShonda D. v. Monroe County Bd. of Educ.*, 526 U.S. 629 (1999), holds that this liability for sexual harassment extends to peer sexual harassment for school-children. School boards and school districts may be liable for such acts, which has led to policies that are designed to be very conservative in avoiding litigation and a federal proposed policy guidance from the Department of Education, regarding peer sexual harassment, 61 Fed. Reg. 42728 (1996). Hence, a kiss may lead to a suspension.

In North Carolina, a six-year-old was suspended from school for kissing a female classmate on the cheek, reported by the *Los Angeles Times*, Sept. 25, 1996, p. A11, that "[u]nwelcome is unwelcome at any age." A week later, a seven-year-old in the second grade was suspended from school for five days in New York, when he kissed a classmate and tore a button from her skirt, as reported by the *Buffalo News*, Oct. 2, 1996, p. A16. The explanation for ripping the button from her clothes was because the bear in his favorite book, "Corduroy" had a missing button. [see Davis v. Monroe County Bd. Of Educ, 526 U.S. 629, 681-682, dissent (1999)].

These sexual harassment cases among the very young, while troubling for many reasons, inspired one lawyer to reflect on his days in elementary school, and a confession about his own experience with a female classmate, with apparent relief that the statute of limitations has run on his incident. This article appeared in the 1996 Tennesee Bar Journal:

Bill Haltom, ***Thank Goodness the Statute has Run on My First Kiss***

I vividly remember my first kiss. It occurred 38 years ago on an autumn day in 1958 in the cloakroom of Mrs. McMurtry's second grade class. I was seven years old and hopelessly in love with a classmate named Kathy. She was an auburn-haired beauty who was the Julia Roberts of our second grade class. For several weeks I had tried desperately to get Kathy's attention. During lunch time I would sit next to her in the school cafeteria, hoping that she and I could share a romantic midday dinner by candlelight. I would open my Roy Rogers lunch box, pull out my thermos bottle with the picture of Roy, Dale and Trigger on the side, and offer Kathy my favorite dessert, a Hostess Twinkie. At recess, I would try to catch Kathy's eye during the kickball game, secretly dedicating each kick to my true love. I even wrote Kathy a love letter, a missive scribbled with one of those huge pencils on tablet paper that featured dotted lines to separate the capital and lower case letters.

Kathy responded to my efforts by doing precisely what women have always done when they want to drive a man crazy. She ignored me. She snubbed me as if I were Ross Perot and she were a member of the Presidential Debate Commission. Of course, this just made me more hopelessly in love with her. I then tried to win her heart by making her laugh. I would cross my eyes for her or try to regale her by doing my imitation of the Three Stooges: "Nyuk! Nyuk! Nyuk!" Kathy never laughed. She never even smiled. She obviously did not share my appreciation of the Three Stooges' dry, understated sense of humor.

And then one morning it happened. I found myself in the cloakroom with Kathy, as we were both removing our canary-yellow school raincoats. I caught a glimpse of Kathy's green eyes, and before I knew it, I just walked up to her and gave her a big juicy kiss, right on the lips. It wasn't just some little wimpy kiss like Prince Charles gave Princess Diana on their wedding day. Nosiree-bob. I kissed Kathy as if she were Scarlett O'Hara and I were Rhett Butler.

I've thought a lot about that first kiss recently as I read the news reports about the six-year-old boy in Lexington, North Carolina, and the seven-year-old boy in New York City, who have both been accused by school bureaucrats of sexual harassment for kissing female classmates.

I guess I'm pretty lucky that it's been 38 years since that first kiss. Although I haven't confirmed this with either Johnny Cochran or Perry Mason, I believe the statute of limitations has run on any sexual harassment suit Kathy might file against me.

No, Kathy never sued me for sexual harassment for that first kiss. She never told Mrs. McMurtry about it, so no school bureaucrat kicked me out of school. But on that autumn day in 1958, Kathy did something more powerful than filing suit or turning me over to school authorities for discipline. What she did was this: shortly after I had given her the big juicy kiss on her lips, Kathy returned the favor by making direct contact with my lips, only she did it with her fist. That's right. Kathy responded to my kiss by giving me a big knuckle sandwich to enjoy along with my Twinkie for lunch that day.

Yes, sweet little Kathy, that delicate flower of Southern womanhood, decked me as if she were Mohammed Ali and I were Barney Fife. And as I picked myself up off the cloakroom floor, I was more in love with her than ever.

I have no idea where Kathy is now. But I'll tell you one thing. I've never gotten over that woman.

The Kiss Goodbye, The Kiss Hello; Kissing, Kissing on the Go

Any man who can drive safely while kissing a pretty girl is simply not giving the kiss the attention it deserves.
---Albert Einstein

In 1656, a kiss "hello" to his wife, Elizabeth meant that Captain Kemble would be punished for two hours in the stocks in Boston, Massachusetts for "lewd and unseemly behavior". Captain Kemble was a wealthy New England merchant, and had been away on a trading trip, when he returned and kissed his wife, Elizabeth at their home's doorway threshold. But because it was "the Sabbath" and because it was in public, the Puritan-inspired law had to be applied, and he spent two hours in the stocks.

Driving While Kissing

In Texas, V.T.C.A., Civil Practice & Remedies Code § 72.001; Chapter 72. Liability of Motor Vehicle Owner or Operator to Guest makes attempts by a rider to hug and kiss the driver, willful misconduct in tort, resulting in liability.

In Ohio's Guest Statute, R.C. § 4515.02, *[T]he owner, operator, or person responsible for the operation of a motor vehicle shall not be liable for loss or damage arising from injuries to or death of a guest, resulting from the operation of said motor vehicle, while such guest is being transported without payment therefor in or upon said motor vehicle, unless such injuries or death are caused by the willful or wanton misconduct of such operator, owner, or person responsible for the operation of said motor vehicle.*

However, in 1956, in Ohio, where a driver was driving the car at a rate of fifty miles-per-hour, while attempting to kiss the guest passenger in the seat beside him, the court found him not guilty of willful or wanton misconduct, under the Ohio Guest Statute. *Davis v. Klaiber,* 229 F.2d 883, 82 Ohio Law Abs. 9 Ohio Op. 2d 414,135 (6th Cir. 1956).

In North Carolina in 1953, the court considered a defense of contributory negligence and proximate cause for injuries claimed by a guest in a car, when the driver left the road and hit a fire hydrant. Both agreed that they were "sharing a kiss" when the auto left the road. The court wrote that the "youthful defendant gave this testimony: 'I ran off the road because she and I were kissing each other . . .. That is the only reason that I was not looking where I was going.'" However, this incident was never mentioned in the defendant's answer.

That being the case, the driver was unable to use the defense of contributory negligence of his passenger who was distracting him from driving with the kissing exchange because he failed to include the affirmative defense of contributory negligence in his answer, required by N.C.G.S. s 1-139 which specifies that *[I]n all actions to recover damages by reason of the negligence of the defendant, where contributory negligence is relied upon as a defense, it must be set up in the answer and proved on the trial. Hunt v. Wooten,* 76 S.E.2d 238 (1953), 326 N.C. 42.

In another North Carolina case, more than fifty years later, another contributory negligence defense arose, where the court held that a passenger was contributorily negligent in her own injuries when the driver of the car, in which she was a guest, had a collision. In this case, the guest was not kissing while the driver was driving the car, but the court found that the guest should have known (or knew) that the *driver was appreciably impaired, because she should have smelled alcohol on [the]driver's breath when he gave her occasional kisses during the evening.* The court found that the guest/passenger and the driver had been together in a drinking establishment for approximately seven hours, and the testimony showed that the guest/passenger knew at the beginning of evening that the driver planned to consume alcohol because they had arranged with the bartender to drive them both home so that they could both consume alcohol. However, at some point the driver decided to drive with a breath test reading of 0.18 determined by a test taken after the collision. The N.C. Court of Appeals held that: (1) the passenger knew or should have known that the motorist was appreciably impaired, and (2) the motorist's intoxication was the proximate cause of the collision. *Taylor v. Coats*, 180 N.C. App. 210, 636 S.E.2d 581 (2006).

Finally, when a Mississippi security patrol officer for a water supply district stopped a motorist allegedly for suspicion of driving under the influence of alcohol (DUI), the court found that he was not acting *in furtherance of the district's interests when he diverted from his employment for personal reasons*, and decided to attempt to kiss the motorist when she was retrieving her driver's license. Because he was not acting within the course and scope of his employment at the time of the attempted kiss, the court found that the water supply district could not be liable under the Mississippi Tort Claims Act, Miss. Code Ann. §11-46-5 Waiver of Immunity. *Cockrell v. Pearl River Valley Water Supply Dist.*, 865 So.2d 357 (Miss. 2004).

Regulating Kissing: Kissing in Mass Transit

When governments regulate, they must have at least do so for a legitimate governmental purpose, rationally related to the means used to regulate. So what is the governmental purpose in regulating kissing? Here, public safety.

While kissing while driving has its own set of public safety problems, mass transit officials in for the Warrington Bank Quay station in the United Kindom were concerned about kissing slowing down the flow of railway passengers from the platforms. The "no kissing" signs went up, and a ban on kissing was instituted. However in Spring 2009, railway officials sensing the unpopularity of their sign, and not wanting to really stop kissing - replaced the no kissing signs with "Kiss Me Quick" signs seen from the platform, and "Kiss Me Longer" signs in the long-term parking area.

The Washington Metro mass transit system has their own version of kissing regulation. In the car lane for dropping off passengers at metro stations around the Washington, D.C. area, a sign prominently displayed directs the passengers to "Kiss and Run".

Kissing on the go is an unavoidable phenomena of human nature, but not one that will escape the Rule of Law.

No kissing sign in the Warrington Bank Quay railway station, United Kingdom railway

Kisses and Guns are not Wine and Roses

A kiss may ruin a human life.
----Oscar Wilde

Unfortunately, we have to get to the unpleasantness of the fatal disasters that can occur when kissing is mixed with guns.

The first reported case in the U.S. occurred in 1873 in frontier Tennessee, when after "amusing himself with a small pistol shooting 'Christmas guns,' the Defendant decided to approach Milley Ford, and demand a kiss. The Defendant had prepared for this prank by loading a paper wad in the gun, rather than a lead bullet, having anticipated her refusal to grant his wish for a kiss. When Milley refused to satisfy his demand for a kiss, he said, 'If you don't kiss me, I will shoot you!' at which point the Defendant put both arms around her and discharged the pistol below her shoulder. Milley fell mortally wounded to the ground, and the Defendant exclaimed, 'For God's sake, forgive me, Milly; I didn't think it would hurt you!'"

The Tennessee Supreme Court reversed his conviction of voluntary homicide, and sent the case back to the trial court to determine whether this was involuntary homicide under the state statute, T. C. A. § 39-13-212. *Criminally negligent homicide. Nelson v. State*, 65 Tenn. 418, (1873).

In North Carolina in 1968, perhaps an even more bizarre incident than the 1873 Tennesse case occurred with guns and kisses. Here, the husband, with his wife sitting on his lap, she bent over to kiss him while the gun was on her finger, and the gun discharged, fatally killing her. *State v. Griffin*, 159 S.E.2d 273 N.C. 333, 889 (1968).

The court opined that it was:

> *defendant's evidence at trial that gun went off while defendant was fondling wife and her arms were around him and that he did not know gun was loaded and had last seen it on arm of chair, tended to show an accidental killing and did not establish that it was defendant who caused the gun to discharge so that his motion for nonsuit made at close of all evidence should have been allowed. Reversed.*

The involuntary manslaughter conviction by the lower court under N.C.G.S. § 14-17. *Murder in the first and second degree defined; punishment*, was reversed on a procedural error in the lower court.

Guns and kisses are not wine and roses.

Hillary kisses Suha at a meeting on November 11, 1999, in Gaza.

The Kiss in Diplomacy (or Lack thereof)

Shirley Temple Black, a U.S. diplomat, reportedly said to a *Times* reporter in 1977 that "over the years, 'I have developed a dart-and-dodge technique to avoid the kiss on the mouth.' She continued to add that 'In diplomatic circles . . . there is a lot of hand kissing.'"

Shirley Temple Black is not the only one to have a diplomatic strategy for a kiss. During a visit to Gaza, November 11, 1999, Hillary Rodham Clinton shared the podium with the Palestinian First Lady, Suha Arafat, and listened to Ms. Arafat's charge that Israel was using toxic gas on the Palestinians and causing miscarriages among pregnant mothers and cancer among the children. Ms. Arafat's husband, Yasser Arafat, had previously stated that, "Our people have been subjected to the daily and extensive use of poisonous gas by the Israeli forces, which has led to an increase in cancer cases among women and children."

In one of the most politically-controversial actions of her senatorial campaign, Hillary Rodham Clinton rose and embraced Mrs. Arafat and kissed her on the cheek. The Israeli Prime Minister was outraged and the American Jewish leaders demanded that Hillary Rodham Clinton respond. Her response was, "I do not believe any kind of inflammatory rhetoric or baseless charges are good for the peace process." The kiss became infamous in the Clinton senatorial campaign.

The Godfather, The kiss of honor

The RICO Kiss, otherwise known in its two forms: the Kiss of Honor and the Kiss of Death

I know it was you Fredo. You broke my heart.
-----The Godfather II
The Godfather (Al Pacino)
as he puts both hands on
either side of his brother's
face (Jon Cazale), and delivers
the "kiss of death"

The Racketeer Influenced Criminal Organizations statute, or RICO, as the law is more popularly known, was passed by Congress as Title IX of the Organized Crime Control Act of 1970. Pub. L. No. 91-452, 84 Stat. 922, codified at 18 U.S.C. and 28 U.S.C. in various sections. Racketeering is defined as follows:

18 U.S.C.A. § 1961

> *(1) "racketeering activity" means (A) any act or threat involving murder, kidnapping, gambling, arson, robbery, bribery, extortion, dealing in obscene matter, or dealing in a controlled substance or listed chemical (as defined in section 102 of the Controlled Substances Act), which is chargeable under State law and punishable by imprisonment for more than one year; (B) any act which is indictable under any of the following [long list of crimes follows]*

In 1987, one of the most important RICO cases was

tried in the United States, *United States v. Gotti*, ending in hugs and kisses among the defendants and their lawyers. The *New York Times* reported on March 14, 1987, the following account:

> *N.Y. Times, Mar. 14, 1987, at 1, col. 1 (nat'l ed.). After a seven-month trial, Gotti and his co-defendants were acquitted of racketeering and conspiracy. They were accused of carrying out illegal gambling and loan-sharking operations, armed hijackings, and at least two murders over an 18-year period.*
> *"Not guilty ... not guilty ... not guilty ..." the jury foreman said over and over again in a low voice. At the defense table, the man described by federal prosecutors as the leader of the nation's most powerful Mafia family smiled and gleefully punched his lawyer on the arm. When the foreman finished his litany, John Gotti and his co-defendants hugged and kissed each other and their lawyers. Then, they stood and applauded as federal marshals escorted the twelve members of the jury from the Brooklyn courtroom.*
> *It was a stunning defeat for the federal prosecutors; the first major courtroom setback in what they described as a campaign to destroy the hierarchy of organized crime in the New York City area. Since 1970, when Congress presented federal prosecutors with a powerful new weapon called the Racketeer Influenced and Corrupt Organizations Act (RICO), prosecutors have recorded a string of successes in major organized-crime cases across the country.*

Andreotti cleared of Mafia conspiracy

A BBC Rome correspondent, David Willey, opined that the Andreotti trial was the most significant political trial in Italy's post-war republic. It was the testimony concerning a meeting where Mr. Andreotti exchanged the kiss of honor with Sicilean mafia boss, Salvatore 'Toto" Riina, in the 1980s, which almost led to his conviction. Mr. Andreotti was accused of being the Godfather of the Rome.

The account of the testimony regarding the kiss, in the *New York Times* during the trial in 1993 describes the kiss of honor:

> *Mr. Di Maggio, a turncoat who betrayed Mr. Riina to the police, said in testimony to Palermo magistrates made public by the Senate today: "I am absolutely certain that I recognized Giulio Andreotti because I saw him many times on television. I interpreted the kiss that Andreotti and Salvatore Riina exchanged as a sign of respect."*
> *According to Mr. Di Maggio's testimony, the incident happened five years ago at the Palermo home of Ignazio Salvo, a high-ranking associate of Mr. Andreotti who was also accused by informers of being one of the politician's main contacts with the mob. Mr. Salvo was murdered last Sept. 17. Another top Sicilian aide to Mr. Andreotti, Salvo Lima, was killed in March 1992. 'Very Serious Slander'*
> *"When we walked in, the people present were the Hon. Giulio Andreotti and the Hon. Salvo Lima," Mr. Di Maggio said, according to the magistrates' account. "They stood up and I*

shook their hand and kissed Ignazio Salvo. Riina, however, greeted with a kiss all three people. I left soon after."

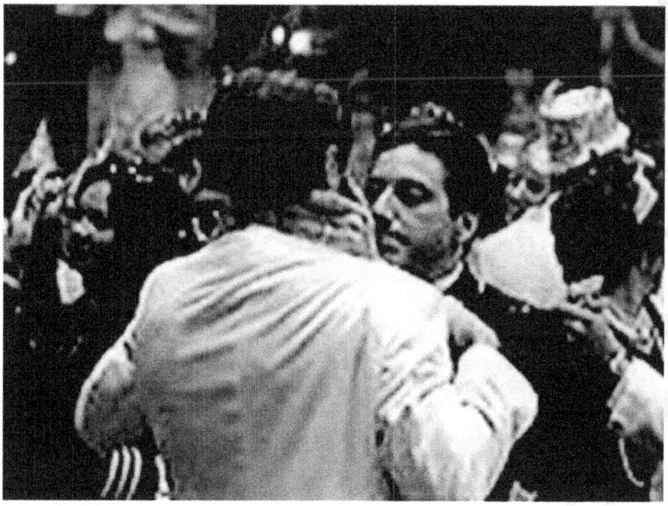

The Godfather II, The kiss of death

HERSHEY'S KISSES

Owning a Kiss in Intellectual Property

Something as iconic as the Hershey Kiss chocolate candy has vast worldwide recognition for the brand and trade dress. The Hershey Kiss was first introduced in 1907 and adopted Kiss and Kisses as trademarks in 1907. From the Hershey's website, the following explanation of the trademarks appears:

> *About HERSHEY'S (R) KISSES(R) Chocolates*
>
> *HERSHEY'S KISSES Brand Chocolates, a little product with a big future, were first introduced in 1907. While it's not known exactly how HERSHEY'S KISSES got their name, it is a popular theory that the candy was named for the sound or motion of the chocolate being deposited during the manufacturing process. Milton S. Hershey, the corporation's founder, established a registered trademark for the "plume" extending out of the wrapper in 1924. A registered trademark for the configuration of HERSHEY'S KISSES is their familiar foil wrap established in 1976.*

The Trademark Electronic Search System of the U.S. Patent and Trademark Office list 16, live, trademark registrations for Hershey's Kisses in various forms shows, the first registered March 16, 1923.

Serial Number	Reg. Number	Word Mark	Check Status	Live/Dead	
1	78842073	3194067	HERSHEY'S KISSES	TARR	LIVE
2	78687580	3363296	SEALED WITH A HERSHEY'S KISS	TARR	LIVE
3	78116813	2757584	HERSHEY'S KISSES	TARR	LIVE
4	77138877		HERSHEY'S KISSES YOU GO! SOCIAL GIRL	TARR	DEAD
5	77137917		HERSHEY'S KISSES YOU GO! SPORTY GIRL	TARR	DEAD
6	77137823		HERSHEY'S KISSES YOU GO! DRAMA GIRL	TARR	DEAD
7	77136493		HERSHEY'S KISSES YOU GO! FASHION GIRL	TARR	DEAD
8	77510925		HERSHEY'S KISSES	TARR	LIVE
9	75304645	2319692	HERSHEY'S KISSMOBILE	TARR	LIVE
10	74489919	1890043	HERSHEY'S HUGS'N KISSES OXOX	TARR	DEAD
11	73721833	1549371	HERSHEY'S KISSES	TARR	LIVE
12	73813948	1587019	HERSHEY'S KISSES	TARR	DEAD
13	73773592	1584608	HERSHEY'S KISSES	TARR	LIVE
14	73714027	1549369	HERSHEY'S KISSES WITH ALMONDS MILK CHOCOLATE	TARR	LIVE
15	73714024	1549368	HERSHEY'S KISSES WITH ALMONDS MILK CHOCOLATE	TARR	LIVE
16	73312292	1236602	HERSHEY'S MILK CHOCOLATE KISSES	TARR	LIVE
17	72284821	0864621	MILK CHOCOLATE HERSHEYS KISSES	TARR	DEAD
18	72284820	0863607	HERSHEY'S KISSES	TARR	LIVE
19	71153982	0165248	HERSHEY'S KISSES	TARR	LIVE
20	71153977	0165247	HERSHEY'S MILK CHOCOLATE KISSES	TARR	DEAD

The company has had to actively defend its trademark over the years, countering arguments that their own trademarks should be cancelled because the word "kiss" was generic at the time Hershey first registered the mark. In a lawsuit, filed in the New Jersey federal district court, April 5, 2007, *Hershey v. Promotion in Motion*, Hershey alleged infringement of its 101-year-old trademark, where Promotion in Motion filed for a trademark registration for SwissKiss, which was introduced in 2005. Hershey argues that the SwissKiss name on chocolate candy "is likely to cause confusion, mistake or deception for purchasers and the consuming public."

Word Mark	**HERSHEY'S KISSES**
Goods and Services	IC 016. US 033 037. G & S: PAPERWEIGHTS. FIRST USE: 19880422. FIRST USE IN COMMERCE: 19880422 IC 021. US 002 033. G & S: ORNAMENTAL CRYSTAL BOWLS WITH LIDS. FIRST USE: 19870904. FIRST USE IN COMMERCE: 19870904 IC 028. US 050. G & S: CHRISTMAS ORNAMENTS. FIRST USE: 19880930. FIRST USE IN COMMERCE: 19880930
Mark Drawing Code	(3) DESIGN PLUS WORDS, LETTERS, AND/OR NUMBERS
Design Search Code	08.03.01 - Candy bars, (chocolate); Chips, (chocolate); Chocolate candies; Chocolate chips 08.03.03 - Wrapped candies (bite size) 26.11.02 - Plain single line rectangles; Rectangles (single line)
Serial Number	73773592
Filing Date	January 9, 1989
Current Filing Basis	1A
Original Filing Basis	1A
Published for Opposition	December 5, 1989
Registration Number	1584608

Registration Date	February 27, 1990
Owner	(REGISTRANT) HERSHEY FOODS CORPORATION CORPORATION DELAWARE 100 MANSION ROAD EAST HERSHEY PENNSYLVANIA 17033 (LAST LISTED OWNER) HERSHEY CHOCOLATE & CONFECTIONERY CORPORATION CORPORATION BY MERGER DELAWARE 5060 WARD ROAD INTELLECTUAL PROPERTY DEPARTMENT WHEAT RIDGE COLORADO 80033
Assignment Recorded	ASSIGNMENT RECORDED
Attorney of Record	MARTHA L. CECIL-FEW
Prior Registrations	0165248;0186828;1038025
Type of Mark	TRADEMARK
Register	PRINCIPAL
Affidavit Text	SECT 15. SECT 8 (6-YR). SECTION 8(10-YR) 20001206.
Renewal	1ST RENEWAL 20001206
Live/Dead Indicator	LIVE

The Legal name, "Kiss" is owned by Hershey Foods, at least when it means a chocolate candy design.

Kissing Animals

The lick of a dog in complete unconditional love for its human companion does not meet our definition of a kiss, but the rule of law must keep our society ordered when humans kiss animals, at least if it is for a public health purpose.

In the early legal history of the United States, however, regulated human interaction with animals was based on morality. Morality was the clear, underlying legislative purpose of the law. In fact, not until *Lawrence v. Texas*, 123 S. Ct. 2472, 2482 (2003), when the U.S. Supreme Court concluded that morality as a basis for law was suspect, and could be unconstitutional, did many existing laws regulating sexuality in states find their end. The prohibition of intimate interaction with animals was originally called the crime of bestiality and found its roots in the description of the interaction between witches and the devil. Even after *Lawrence*, which called into question the legislative effort to regulate sexuality, still, 24 states have laws prohibiting bestiality and 15 of these states' laws are felonies. But it is not a kiss alone that will find you afoul of these laws.

However, a kiss at least to a reptile is considered a serious public health concern, and indeed, small children who kiss their pet turtles could acquire a sometimes deadly salmonellosis infection from the bacteria which live on reptiles.

In Illinois, the law requires a specific notice to purchasers or recipients of reptiles, warning them not to kiss their pet

reptile, and the notice is proscribed exactly as it is to appear to potential purchasers or recipients of reptiles. Specifically the notice shall be: "Don't nuzzle or kiss your pet reptile." *225 ILCS 605/18.1 § 18.1. Sale or gift of reptiles and other animals.*
(a) A pet shop shall not sell a reptile, offer a reptile for sale, or offer a reptile as a gift or promotional consideration unless a notice regarding safe reptile-handling practices that meets the requirements in subsection (b) is (i) prominently displayed at each location in the pet shop where reptiles are displayed, housed, or held and (ii) distributed to the purchaser or recipient.
(b) The notice regarding safe reptile-handling practices shall be one of the following:
. . . (D) "Don't nuzzle or kiss your pet reptile."

Fortunately, the Princess in The Frog Prince, was able to kiss the frog and release him from his spell, without running afoul of any law in the late 1800s, prohibiting kissing an amphibian!

Seven-year-old Sambath Uon kisses his pet python.
Dailymail.com

Kissing Law Trivia

The States of Kissing

Indiana: it is illegal for a mustached man to "habitually kiss human beings"

Hartford, Connecticut: a husband is prohibited from kissing his wife on Sunday.

To "Kiss and Make Up" may be a cavalier supervisory directive

The Illinois Human Rights Commission found a cavalier attitude where a supervisor told an employee that he and a male employee who was harassing him "should kiss and make up". The supervisor was aware of the sexual situation between the two employees and later asked whether they had "kissed and made up." The Commission found a "cavalier attitude" but did not go as far as finding it illegal. *Pinnacle Ltd. Partnership v. Illinois Human Rights Com'n*, App. 4 Dist.2004, 290 Ill. Dec. 139, 354 Ill.App.3d 819, 820 N.E.2d 1206

"Kiss my foot" is a non-acceptance

The Iowa Uniform Commercial Code § 3-410. Definition and Operation of Acceptance, generally recognizes that a signature of the drawee alone is sufficient for the acceptance of commercial paper. Nothing more is needed, such as "accepted" or "certified" – simply a signature. However, if there are any other words indicating an intent NOT to accept the commercial paper, then it does not constitute an acceptance. The Iowa court held that such was the case when a drawee signature included the words "kiss my foot", indicating a rejection, in *Norton v. Knapp*, 64 Iowa 112, 19 N.W. 867 (1884).

"Kiss our boys for me", established paternity

In the Iowa, a child can inherit from its biological father but only where evidence proving paternity is available during the father's lifetime or if the child is recognized by the father. A message sending a kiss was sufficient for inheriting the biological father's estate, where the father had written to the mother of the boys, requesting that she "kiss our boys for me." Rules of Inheritance; Sec. 633.222. Biological child--inherit from father; *Brown v. Iowa Legion of Honor*, 107 Iowa 439, 78 N.W. 73, (1899).

Global Kissing and the Law

London: It is illegal in London to kiss a girl on a Sunday.

Italy: Kissing in public is only legal at railroad stations.

Germany: Kissing is illegal in trains.(in 1912)

Australia: Under the age of 16 years of age, two people, no more than 3 years different in age, are permitted to kiss.

Malaysia: Kissing is illegal in taxis.

Censorship of the Kiss in India

Kissing censorship has a deep history in India. Under British rule, the Indian Cinematographic Act in 1918 introduced mandatory licensing of movie theaters, but this was primarily a control mechanism over artistic material that may have influenced the citizenry in a way that was not conducive to British rule. During this time, however, a kiss or kissing in films was not forbidden by the censors. Post-British rule, and the establishment of the Indian government in 1947, the tradition of review continued, but it became more centralized. In 1952, a new Indian Cinematographic Act was passed which continued the review and censorship function of the government. It was in implementation of this Act that a "kissing ban" was enacted, created by the Censorship Board. In 1960, the Cinematographic Censorship rules were promulgated, which were a set of guidelines for certifying films that could be shown in theaters. In 1978, the guidelines were revised but with more conceptual standards, requiring that the film be judged in general, rather than for specific performing elements, for example, where "human sensibilities are not offended by vulgarity, obscenity and depravity."

Interestingly, kissing other parts of the body is acceptable in films and can be shown, and foreign films which include kissing are not held to the same standards and are often certified. Directors of Indian films have developed ways to get around the ban with cinematic mechanisms, such as kissing an object, like a pillow, suggestive dancing, or having only partial views of the actors and actresses, behind buildings or trees. The "wet sari scene" is often used as a substitution for the kissing scene, which reveals every curve of the wearer. Even with the modern liberal censorship standards, kissing is still fairly rare in Indian films because of this long traditional of censorship, and the backlash for a passionate kissing scene might be too risky.

Recently an American actor, Richare Gere, while appearing in India with a well-known Indian actress, Shilpa Shetty of Bollywood fame, while on stage, passionately kissed her in a full embrace she arched backward. The report from CNN, April 19, 2007 with photos, appeared as follows:

> ***Gere and Shetty Face Legal Action Over Public Kiss***
> *Actor Richard Gere and Bollywood beauty Shilpa Shetty are facing legal action in India after being accused of committing "an obscene act" last weekend. The Chicago star swept the popular Bollywood actress into his arms and kissed her several times during an AIDS-awareness event last weekend, with angry crowds burning effigies of Gere for going too far in a country where such public*

displays of affection are largely taboo.

Three lawyers in India have now filed complaints against their amorous actions, and Shetty, along with several private television channels, face two further charges for showing videos of the kiss after legal papers were filed in Ghaziabad. Shetty, who publicly defended Gere on Tuesday, says she is paying a price for being an international celebrity. Her spokesperson says, "The media should concentrate on the promotion of the cause of AIDS awareness rather than making an issue out of kisses."

AP reported the litigation news:

NEW DELHI (AP) — Three lawyers filed complaints in Indian courts against actor Richard Gere and Bollywood actress Shillpa Shetty for kissing at a public function, a news report said Wednesday.

In his complaint, attorney Poonal Chandra Bhandari accused the actors of committing "an obscene act" in a public place, which India's conservative society cannot tolerate, Press Trust of India said.

Two other lawyers filed another complaint in a court in Ghaziabad, a town on the outskirts of the Indian capital, against Shetty and private television channels for showing videos of the kissing incident, the news agency added.

Such cases against celebrities — often filed by publicity seekers — are common in conservative India. They add to a backlog of legal cases in the country that has nearly crippled the judicial system.
The complaints filed Tuesday came a day after angry crowds in several Indian cities burned effigies of Gere after he wrapped Shetty in his arms and kissed her several times on her cheeks during an AIDS awareness event in the Indian capital.

On Tuesday, Magistrate Dinesh Chandra Gupta, in the northwestern Indian city of Jaipur, ordered private television news channel NDTV to provide the original videotape of the incident by next week, the Press Trust of India news agency said.

Chief Judicial Magistrate Reena Chaudhry said she would hear that complaint on April 18.

Photographs of Gere, 57, embracing Shetty, 31, and kissing her on the cheek were splashed across front pages of newspapers Monday in India — a country where public displays of affection are largely taboo.

Shetty tried to end the controversy by saying that the hug and the kiss were not obscene and that the public was overreacting.

On Wednesday, her representative, Dale Bhagwagar, declined comment on the court complaints but said Shetty was paying a price for being an international celebrity.

"The media should concentrate on the promotion of the cause of AIDS awareness rather than making an issue out of kisses," Bhagwagar told The Associated Press.

Judge Dinesh Gupta reviewed footage of Gere and Shetty in this act of kissing and issued an arrest warrant for Gere and a summons for Shetty, after determining that the act violated India's obscenity law. Shortly thereafter, Judge Gupta was transferred to a new court, several hours away.

By May 2007, the Supreme Court of India suspended the arrest warrant for Richard Gere, and suspended the legal proceedings while an interlocutory proceeding was held to determine whether the Supreme Court had proper jurisdiction to hear the case. Shetty petitioned the court to transfer the case from Jaipur to Mumbai, her hometown.

Apparently, Gere was entertaining the truckers at the AIDS awareness event, by re-enacting a scene from his film, *Shall We Dance.*

Pakistan

Pakistan also prohibits kissing in films, and went so far as to impose a fine on Meera, an actress who performed a kissing scene in an Indian Bollywood movie, *Nazar*, in February 2005. Purportedly, in reaction to this incident, the Pakistani government in Islamabad considered banning all Pakistani actors from appearing in Indian movies.

President Ahmadinejad's Public Kiss

One of the most devout disciples of conservative Islam, President Ahmadinejad, was accused of violating Islamic law when he apparently could not resist kissing the hand of his former primary school teacher at a reunion. The following report from the United Kingdom captured the outrage of this act.

> *May 30, 2007* ***Iran***
> ***Anger at kiss for teacher***
> *Richard Beeston*
> *He has championed the cause of the most extreme movements in Islam and cast himself as the devout disciple of the late Iranian revolutionary leader, Ayatollah Khomeini.*
>
> *But President Ahmadinejad of Iran yesterday found himself accused of breaking Islamic law with an "indecent" public act, after he could not resist embracing and kissing the hand of his former primary school teacher, an elderly woman, at an impromptu reunion.*
>
> *"This type of indecency has grave consequences, like violating religious and sacred values," thundered the conservative*

Hezbollah newspaper, which described the incident as unprecedented in the 28-year Iranian revolution. Islamic law forbids men touching women to whom they are not related. Although in private these rules are often ignored by Iranians, strict adherence by officials is expected.

There is concensus in Islamic Law about kissing. Males and females do not kiss unless they are related by blood or marriage, and same-gender kisses are acceptable as long as they are done without lust and the mouths do not meet. Kisses may be placed on the hands and cheeks, as well as the forehead, because the Prophet Mohammad is said to have placed a kiss on a man's forehead in one instance.

Islam and the Kiss of Life

Mouth to mouth resusitation, sometimes referred to as the "kiss of life," is considered to be permissible under Islamic law, but only if it is necessary and done without "lust".

The Russian Wedding Kiss

A center piece of the Russian wedding is a long, sustained kiss between the newly married couple, performed at the behest of the guests who demand they continue kissing as long as they count. All the guests count together "1 – 2 – 3 – 4 – 5 – 6 – 7 -8, etc." while the couple stands and continues kissing. This is initiated by a cry of "gor' ko" until the couple begins the sustained kiss. This can happen many times during the wedding reception, and the longer they kiss the stronger the union is perceived to be by the guests. While this is not a legal requirement, the tradition has become inextricably linked with the legal aspect of the ceremony.

Bibliography

1. Introduction

Page 2
Andrea Demirjian, *Kissing: Everything you ever wanted to know about one of life's sweetest pleasures* (Perigree Trade, 2006).

Page 2
Cambridge International Dictionary of Idioms © Cambridge University Press 1998

2. Some important scientific facts about kissing

Page 6
Chip Walter, *Affairs of the Lips: Why We Kiss,* Scientific American Mind Magazine, Scientific American, January 31, 2008.

Irenaus Eibl-Eibesfeldt, Love and Hate: The Natural History of Behavior Patterns (1970).

3. The kiss: The sacred to the secular

Kiril Petkov, *The Kiss of Peace*; and Karen Harvey, ed., *The Kiss in History,* Manchester University Press (2005).

George von Rautenfeld, Nonverbal Communication in the "Nibelungenlied" Compared with that in the "Chanson de Roland" and the "Poema de Mio Cid" 104-05 (1980) (unpublished Ph.D. dissertation, University of Maryland) (suggesting that in early medieval Germany, it may have been the responsibility of the offender to initiate the kiss).

4. **A Kiss is just a Kiss, except when it is worth a lot of money**
Mendonsa v. Time Incorporated, 678 F.Supp. 967 (D.R.I. 1988)

J. Michael Kennedy, "The Kiss Seen "Round the World," The Los Angeles Times, 8/22/05 L.A. Times (Bus. Sec.). [the Eisenstaedt photograph interviews]

Adrienne Blue called *On Kissing: From the Metaphysical to the Erotic* (London: Victor Gollancz, 1996) [the Paris kiss story]

France, "French Verdict: Kiss Dismissed," *New York Times*, June 3, 1993

5. **The Celebrated Contractual Kisses**
Quoted story about Finch v. Waters, Newbern, North Carolina: "An Important Case," *New York Times* (May 12, 1880).

John D. Lawson, ed., *The Central Law Journal*, Case Summaries, Vol. XI, July to Dec. 1880, p. 160, published by Soule, Thomas & Wentworth (1880). (Original at Princeton University)

Irish Law Times and Solicitors' Journal: A Weekly Gazette of Legal Postings, Vol. XIV, p. 358 (1880).

Restatement (Second) of Contracts (2008), Copyright © 1981-2008 by the American Law Institute.

6. **Kisses and the Konstitution [sic]**

7. **Is a Kiss "any other valuable inducement" in elections?**
26 Am Jur 2d Elections § 380 (1996)

Elaine Chalus, "Kisses for votes: the kiss and corruption in eighteenth-century English elections, Karen Harvey, ed., *The Kiss in History*, pp. 122-147 (University of Manchester Press, 2008).

John Trusler, The Country Election(London, 1768, 1788) cited by Chalus at fn5.

Oregon Rep. Party v. State, 78 Or.App. 601, 604-05 (Or.App. 1986)

Lance Morrow, "The Great Kissing Epidemic," Time Magazine (Mon., Feb. 7, 1977) at http://www.time.com/time/magazine/article/0,9171,914776,00.html

8. **Kiss and Tell**
Famous quotation source:
William Congreve, Love for Love 48 (Malcolm Kelsall ed., W.W. Norton & Co. 1999) (1695)

Kiss and Tell: Protecting Intimate Relationship Privacy Through Implied Contracts of Confidentiality, 74 UCINLR 887 (Spring 2006).

9. The Forbidden Kiss: Indiscriminate Gender Kissing

Stephanie Francis Cahill, Prisoner of Love Fights for Rights: Gay Inmate's Partner Challenges Arizona Prisons' No-Kissing Rule , ABA Journal E-Report August 23, 2002. Copyright © 2002 American Bar Association; Stephanie Francis Cahill.

Donald H.J. Hermann, Legal Incorporation and Cinematic Reflections of Psychological Conceptions of Homosexuality, 70 UMKC L. Rev. 495 (Spring, 2002). Copyright (c) 2002 by Curators of the University of Missouri; Donald H.J. Hermann.

10. Kiss the Bible, Or Not

E. Cobham Brewer's *Dictionary of Phrase and Fable*, published in 1898.

Photo, Life Magazine, Newly appointed Secretary of State James F. Byrnes (C) kissing the Bible at the swearing in ceremony as President Harry S. Truman (R) watches. Location: Washington, DC, US ;

Date taken: July 1945; Photographer: George Skadding

11. Order in the Court

Kiril Petkov, *The Kiss of Peace*; and Karen Harvey, ed., *The Kiss in History*, Manchester University Press (2005).

Washington v. Judge Alaimo, 934 F. Supp. 1395 (S.D.Ga. 1996)

State v. Law, Unpublished Opin. No. 2007-UP-557

12. The Unwanted Kiss

13. The Kiss Goodbye, The Kiss Hello;
Kissing, Kissing on the Go

"The Privy Council and Colonial Courts," 7 Law Notes (Edward Thompson Co.) 41, 44 (1903-1904) Issue 3 (June 1903).

14. Kisses and Guns are not Wine and Roses

15. The Kiss in Diplomacy

Lance Morrow, "The Great Kissing Epidemic," Time Magazine (Mon., Feb. 7, 1977) at http://www.time.com/time/magazine/article/0,9171,914776,00.html

16. The RICO Kiss

BBC, Saturday, October 23, 1999 available at, http://news.bbc.co.uk/2/hi/europe/483029.stm.

Alan Cowell, "Andreotti and Mafia: A Kiss Related," New York Times, April 21, 1993 at http://query.nytimes.com/gst/fullpage.html?res=9F0CE7D7163DF932A15757C0A965958260 .

17. Owning a Kiss in Intellectual Property

http://www.thehersheycompany.com/news/release.asp?releaseID=437307

Hugh R. Morley, Closter firm asks Hershey: Isn't A Kiss just a Kiss? NorthJersey.com, Friday, October 17, 2008 at http://www.northjersey.com/business/news/Closter_firm_asks_Hershey_Isnt_a_kiss_just_a_kiss.html .

18. Kissing Animals

Michael Roberts, *The Unjustified Prohibition Against Bestiality: Why the Laws in Opposition Can Find No Support Under the Harm Principle*, (Aug 2008) Electronic copy available at: http://ssrn.com/abstract=1328310.

19. **Kissing Trivia**
Questions about states odd kissing laws:
Paul D. Healey, *De Minimis Curat Lex: A Compendium of Legal Trivia*, 89 Law Libr. J. 55 (Winter, 1997)

Must Not Kiss in Trains, *The New York Times* (September 26, 1912).

20. **Global Kissing and the Law**
Gere and Shetty Face Legal Action Over Public Kiss, WENN April 19, 2007 http://www.wenn.com/ .
Richard Beeston, "*Anger at kiss for teacher,*" *TimesOnline UK*, May 30, 2007.

Made in the USA
Monee, IL
04 November 2026

67377644R00075